# MY SALES PERSPECTIVE

A MUST READ FOR ALL SALES PROFESSIONALS

**MY SALES PERSPECTIVE**
**A must read for all sales professionals**

Copyright © 2024 by AYO OGIDAN
ISBN-9798332546778

Published in Nigeria by
TESTIMONY PUBLISHING HOUSE

This Book must not be copied or printed for commercial gain or profit without written permission from Ayo Ogidan

For permission requests, enquiries, consultations, training requests. Please send to:
Instagram: @ayoogidan
Instagram: @souqgrandeur
Whatsapp: +2348157313120

TESTIMONY PUBLISHING HOUSE
PG Quarters, Covenant University, Ota, Nigeria
Tel:+2348088645545
Email: testimonypublishinghouse@gmail.com

# Other Books by the same Author

**The Monkey of Onikoko**
Available on amazon

**Horrors of a Dog Bite**
Available on amazon

# TABLE OF CONTENT

**Chapter 1**
ARE YOU A SALES PROFESSIONAL OR NOT     1

**Chapter 2**
MY JOURNEY FROM SUB - PRIME TO PRIME PROPERTIES     11

**Chapter 3**
THE JOURNEY TO SALES IS TOUGH AS NAILS     17

**Chapter 4**
QUALITIES OF A GOOD SALES PERSON     27

**Chapter 5**
UNDERSTANDING THE SALSES PROCESSES     37

**Chapter 6**
MARKETING IS LIKE THROWING A PARTY     47

**CONCLUSION**     53

# ACKNOWLEDGEMENT

It would be a sin for me to proceed into this book without acknowledging those who represent the core of my very being. As you may have guessed, I'll like to start with my ever beautiful, loving and supportive wife; Ayomide for always having my back through the awesome, good and not so good time. I love you babe and I always will. My kids are an inspiration to me any day. Each time I look at them, I see love beyond what I can even describe.

How can I forget my mum and are continuous prayers and words of encouragement. I could never have asked for a better mother. I love you ma. I tell people all the time that my siblings are the best. They are ever so supportive, especially you Dolapo (my kid sister). Thank you for always being so awesome.

And to everyone who has taught me a lesson or two in this amazing school called life; I say a very big thank you and God bless.

# INTRODUCTION

It is a known fact that most people detest sales jobs. Nobody wants to sell but they all want to be paid. Entrepreneurs want to start up their companies but feel it is not really that important to master the art of selling, since they think they can always employ some graduates to comb the streets and do the dirty work for them. I wish it was that easy. If only you knew that nobody will ever be able to sell your product better than you as a business owner. If your sales team or your head of sales can do a better job than you in selling your products, you have failed and you will always be at their mercy, since the person bringing in the money is the boss of those spending it.

As observed in today's corporate settings, you have MD's that come straight from Harvard or some other fancy school to head organizations but they know almost nothing about practical sales. Their only qualification is that their daddies are either major shareholders in the firm or out rightly own the firms. No wonder these companies struggle to achieve sales. My Sales Perspective is a book on my journey so far as a salesman with over 20 years of very practical experience. In this book I shared about my struggles as well as my victories. I also tried to deal with the different mind sets hindering both organizations and sales individuals from achieving their desired results in sales.

Most times in sales, the battle is lost right at the starting line. Hence, your starting point is where you require the most concentration of energy. The goal of this book is to help you the reader achieve 'lift up' in your career as sales professional and keep soaring for as long as you so desire. I also tried to address the unhealthy attitudes of organizations towards their sales force so that together, we can all make progress.

Happy reading!

CHAPTER 1

# ARE YOU A SALES PROFESSIONAL OR NOT

# ARE YOU A SALES PROFESSIONAL OR NOT

I have been asked by many people about how I would describe myself. They mostly wanted to know if I see myself as a realtor or as a salesman (even though a realtor is also a sales professional but one who focuses only on real estate). Now, considering the way people feel generally about sales representatives (they are seen as con men who would deceive customers just to sell their products) I didn't want to be seen mainly as a sales man. I preferred to be recognized as a real estate professional since it's sort of more specialized than the general sales professional. However, after a careful review of my past works and the paths I have taken in my professional career, I came to the obvious conclusion that, I'm a salesman.

I realized that I have sold a lot of items over a 20 year period. I've sold cars (for my dad and uncle), books and compact discs (immediately after graduation), tie and dye fabrics as well as waste bags (which I sold during my National Youth Service in Kebbi State), Frozen foods (started this after my service to the nation and it sustained me till I got a regular job), Airway manuals and navigational charts, Aviation training programs, IATA & ICAO publications, Ideas/proposals, fashion accessories (including bags, shoes etc) and in the past 12 years I've sold real estate.

I am proud of all these because I love to sell. I feel very fulfilled when I make a sale but much more than my sales of all these items, the most valuable product I have managed to sell most successfully over the years is the brand Ayo Ogidan (my brand).

Until you discover the art of selling yourself as a person to everyone you come across, you cannot succeed as a salesman. The products you sell are temporary and transient in nature but you will always remain the constant factor. You must love yourself and treat yourself well all the time because if shop 'YOU' should close up, that's the end of sales of any sort from that outlet. It's also extremely important to note that people buy you first before they consider what you're trying to sell them. So, dress well, smell nice, speak right and confidently when you're with customers.

My experience from sales of all these items though is that the more expensive the products you're selling are; the more resilient you have to be.

**MY FIRST OFFICIAL SALE JOB**
I often wonder why the sales team in most companies are some of the worst treated departments in these organisations. My first formal job was in the aviation industry. I was hired as a sales executive to sell, Jeppesen Airway manuals/GPS cards, ICAO publications, IATA training programs etc. My department wasn't the highest grossing department in the company but it was the 3rd highest money making department in the company with an unlimited potential (especially because of its training arm). The structure of the company was such that the number of staff in the cost centers was like three times the size of the sales teams in the various business divisions.

The Managing Director of the company for some reason thought it wise to put staff he has sexual relations with in key positions (like the General Manager Administration, General Manager Finance, Human Resources etc) because he is (I understand the situation is still the same) convinced that he can trust them and they are somehow invested in him as a person. He also believes that they would be more stable in terms of career movements (since they're pretty much unqualified for the offices they hold and they are over reliant on him) and that they areand would remain loyal to him. It was such a mess back then as there were sometimes cold war going on amongst them in the office while the work suffered.

I believe in empowering women but I think a lot of emphasis should be placed on their competency and professionalism. As expected, we soon started feeling like slaves to the cost centers (which includes the Administration, the Finance and Human resources departments and headed by these jokers) and in no time, employee turnover in the firm went through the roof. These cost centers made the rules that governed our activities (including penalties), they were always so quick to jump on our case and start criticizing whenever sales wasn't coming; they made a bunch of bureaucratic rules that made even internal processing of resources for the purpose of work so difficult and frustrating.

So, it became a constant case of us going out to hustle for sales and these folks (who sat down in their offices all day and knew very little about our challenges in the market) would pester us either about some rule we had just broken or how we were late on the submission of some really mundane document. To make matters worse, promotion and reward of these cost centers were more rapid than ours because the company believed that they were the ones working (keeping the rest of us in check) and since the rest of us were just there to do whatever we were told to do, our career growth was slow paced. In some instances, sales people were placed on contract while staff of other divisions had permanent employment. I remember this being a very frustrating period for me so, I didn't stay long there. I resigned after 2 years even though I didn't have an alternative job at the time.

I remember this being a very frustrating period for me so, I didn't stay long there. I resigned after 2 years even though I didn't have an alternative job at the time.

The experience of many sales people in African and other developing countries is very similar to this. These companies place very little value on the sales and marketing departments even though the revenue for the entire company is expected to come from sales. They threaten nonperforming the sales staff with sack while the highly performing staff are offered very little reward. It's not enough to continually preach to the sales department that they are the engine room of the company; I believe we must treat them like they are. Some of these ill treatments of sales teams by organizations are powered by some fundamental beliefs of management. Negative Marketing/Sales Beliefs by Organizations

The following are some of the reasons why companies don't invest is their marketing/sales departments:

1. **Our product sells itself:** This is a myth. Products are not bought, they are sold.
2. All we have to do is advertise and customers will come: Selling is a process that takes time. Advertising give you awareness, not sales
3. We can't afford to spend money on sale people.

We'll rather invest in production: What is the use of producing if you can't sell what you're producing? It's just like cooking a lot of food and having no one to eat and appreciate your cooking.

4. **We have no competitors:** This statement is not complete. It should be; 'we don't have competitors yet'. It is a guarantee that someone or a group of people are already planning on taking the market and most (if not all) your customers from you. With this attitude, it's just a matter of time before more serious companies take that market over.

5. **Everybody likes our brand:** One of the harshest truths in the world of sales is that there is no such thing as a loyal customer. The perceived like or love of your brand right now is only because there is probably no better alternative yet. Once there is, you would see that the perceived love/like was never really there.

6. **We have this industry on lock down:** Many organizations have said this in the past but most of them are no longer in existence today. Companies who have this belief are treading on really dangerous grounds as it may lead them to start taking a lot of things for granted (including their customers). This would be fast tracked if you don't have a good sales

force giving your firm firsthand information about the changing needs and wants of your customers.

## Negative Attitude of Sales Executives towards Sales

More important than how organizations see sale men and women is how they see themselves. Not many people are proud of this profession. Most take on sales jobs for lack of other options and while on the job, they're constantly looking for other roles that don't come with the dreaded monthly targets or queries that come with non performance.

In my opinion, one of the major problems people have about sales is attitudinal. Most sales employees fail on the jobs even before they start. And that is because they don't believe in themselves or in their abilities to sell.

CHAPTER 2

# MY JOURNEY FROM SUB - PRIME TO PRIME PROPERTIES

# MY JOURNEY FROM SUB - PRIME TO PRIME PROPERTIES

I remember when I decided to migrate from the subprime Real estate market to selling luxury and Ultra luxury properties. While selling low end real estate, I often wondered how it would feel to sell properties to the super-wealthy folks in the country and where one might meet these people. According to statistics, there are 12, 300 billionaires in Nigeria (as against the 60, 000 billionaires in Mumbai alone) whose sources of wealth are of verifiable routes. These numbers of course are more likely to decrease than increase in a country like this. Now imagine how tricky it would be to look for people like these out of a population of almost 200 million. Finding them however is one thing, getting them to buy what you're selling is another. Most of them will tell you that they would rather build themselves than buy already built properties which would have been highly marked up.

Despite this situation, I wanted so badly to know what it would feel like to sell such properties and would regularly dream of meeting one of such wealthy people (Since I had never met any before). I got so passionate about that when my then colleagues talked bad about how developers of such properties were wasteful and ill advised, I was quick to jump to their defense and justify the logic behind building for the billionaires amongst us. My chance came in 2008, in form of a marketing executive job for one of such development companies that specialized in building luxury and ultra-luxury building in Ikoyi, Lagos (where you have the most expensive properties in Africa and most parts of Europe). You see, I discovered long ago that you cannot attract what you constantly speak against and I believe with a doubt that it was my constant talk and defense of developers like this that took me to them.

Like I knew I would, I passed the interview stages in flying colors and the last stage was a meeting with 3 of the main directors (including the chairman) of the company. Two of them loved me and believed I could do the job effectively but one of them was greatly concerned for me. He kept asking me to explain to him how I intended to sell their properties (which was an average of between $1 million to $2.5 Million)when the average price of the properties I was used to selling was around N5 million ($13, 700) –N8 million ($21,917). It was a very hard question for me to answer, the truth was that I didn't know how I would be able to achieve such feat myself and all through my interviews with them, I hadn't really thought through. All I had was faith that I could do it. However, faith like hope is not a strategy and I dare not mention something that ridiculous to a man like that who believe mostly in logic and strategies.

I paused for a minute (all eyes on me) looked the man in the eyes and responded. My response was: 'sir, you're right to be concerned, but I'm not afraid of this challenge. I came into the real estate sector with no prior experience or mentorship but I was determined to learn and succeed. People may fail, but principles don't and I am confident that the same principles I engaged to sell my N5 to N8 million houses will guide me through these ones. I know the behavioral patterns of these clients may differ a bit (because of the class bridge) however, in the end, people are people and we all want the same thing which is to be happy.' I don't think my answer convinced him about me, but I think it made him willing to give me a chance.

So, I got the job. Doing the job however, was a different story entirely. Like the doubtful man thought, it was very challenging experience for me. I had nobody in my circle who knew any very wealthy client that could help me out. They only prayed for me and wished me well. But I didn't give up; I kept at it and maintained my optimism on a daily basis despite my many disappointments.

CHAPTER 3

# THE JOURNEY TO SALES IS TOUGH AS NAILS

# THE JOURNEY TO SALES IS TOUGH AS NAILS

After about 6 months of working at this new company, I had made zero sales and leased out only one condo. I was really scared and worried. My Managing Director called me into his office one day and he gave me a piece of his mind. He told me of the high hopes he had when employing me and how I was a total disappointment. If I felt scared and concerned before that day, all my fears became magnified exponentially. At this point, it was clear that my sack was imminent. Getting up every morning to go to work became more difficult but despite all my fears and insecurities, I decided to give it my all.

The company employed two of us on the same day; the other guy is an architect by profession but was employed as a marketer/sales executive as well. After realizing that he couldn't do the job, he started lobbying with people at the head office for a transfer to the projects department, but all his attempts yielded zero results. He was stuck and didn't know what else to do so, he would stay in the office all day and play on the internet or go out to see his friends under the guise of marketing. He had given up, he was only trying at that point to enjoy himself while he looked for another job.

Not long after my horrible meeting with the MD, I started making friends in the industry who had the kind of clients I was looking for and they encouraged be not to give up. They also helped me and I started making some leases (these were small amounts and I was still considered as a nonperforming staff). One of the things I did quite well during this time was to make friends with all the facilities personnel in the estates and gave them my complementary cards with instruction to call me directly if any one came to make enquiries at any of the estates. It was a very wise move and my effort paid off eventually.

I got a call from one of the estate electricians one day that a client was at one of the estates and was asking some questions. I didn't have an official car then so, I hoped on a bike and hurried to Ikoyi from my office in V.I.

I met with the man and we started talking. He wanted to buy a four bedroom maisonette but his offer and condition was peculiar. The best price for each of the units was about N220 million ($1.375 million) back then but the buildings were not fully completed yet. He had a total of N160 Million ($1 million) with him and offered to buy the property in carcass form just as it was and complete same by himself.

This was going to be a difficult transaction to pull offas it would mean that the company would be letting go of over $375, 000 from the total sales price. I collected the client's details and promised to get back to him. I had sold the property to the client; the challenge now was to sell his proposal to management. I got to the office and instantly started looking at the different scenarios under which this offer would fly. I called my colleagues at the projects department and started trying to estimate the cost of completing the apartment from the stage it was at the moment vis a vis the $375, 000 that the company may seemingly lose if they were to accept the client's offer. I put together some details, prayed and marched into my MD's office.

I tabled the matter before him (my MD) and I could see

he was excited about it, he asked about the client's details and I gave it to him. He asked me to call the man and set up a meeting for him, I guess he was trying to see if he could push the client to do better on his offer but the man insisted. Again, we promised to get back to the client and he (my MD) escalated the matter to the chairman and other board members. After much deliberation, their answer was a NO. They instructed that I go back to the client and tell him that the property would be completed in a matter of months but that he could deposit the N160 million he had and pay the outstanding balance later. I passed the message across to the client and he also said NO, that was his final offer.

At this point, I knew I had to be smart of else I would lose the transaction. For them, it was easy to say no and move on but for me, if I failed to close this transaction, my job would remain threatened. I made up my mind to close the deal at all cost. So, I decided to go and see each of the directors individually and sell the idea to them before they met to deliberate on the matter again. Starting with my MD, I met the other 5 directors but didn't have access to the chairman so; I invested all my efforts on the other Directors. They all promised to think about it but I didn't let them rest. To cut the long story short, after their meeting, the chairman decided to do something he never does. He asked me to set up a meeting between him and the client. This was very good for me. He was going to offer the man a final price of N200 million after which they would close on the matter but I knew even that wouldn't work. So, I went to meet the client and coached him on how we were going to win this battle. I armed him the right ammunition (information) and told him from which angle to attack. I was present at the meeting (although I wasn't there to speak but to observe), it went awesomely well. The client promised to give referrals, and give us links to some companies we had been trying to reach and also to some of his rich friends. The chairman kept smiling throughout the meeting, he had made a new friend and I had met my first very rich client and made my first sale. After the meeting, everything else was just formalities, the client paid and I became a star while my colleague was asked to resign.

Following this sale, my confidence level went up and somehow things started to change for me, I found that I was now closing more leases (in USD) and before long, the attention of the head office was on me. The chairman started asking questions about me and soon he asked that I be transferred from my office to work directly with him. This was after my forth year at the company. I worked with him for three years and in that time, I sold about 5 more properties of between $1.3 million and $1.67 million and a pent house (which was the highlight for me) of $5 million. I also closed so many leases almost totaling $10 million (excluding lease renewals) but like the story is for most salesmen in this country, even though I was closing these deals and making these huge sums for the company, it didn't reflect in my life as an individual. I had been made head of marketing but my income and standard of living didn't reflect what I was selling.

I still lived in Alapere (a low end of town) even though I worked and sold properties on the Island (Ikoyi and Victoria Island).Although the company had many properties, I was never even offered a BQ in any of them much less the option of owning any. The company was making good money but I didn't even have an official car.

I had an old Toyota corolla for a departmental pool car (which I wasn't even allowed to take home) and despite the fact that most of my target market were living on the Island, I stayed far away from them in a location where our paths could never cross and I was still expected to perform and rise to the company's financial needs month-in, month-out.

I think the most frustrating part of it for me, was the fact that as head of marketing, everyone looked at me when there was no money and I took the heat when it was hard to pay salaries. Also, no matter how much money the sales team made, it was never enough. If we brought in a really large amount of money, it would buy me at most, two weeks break from the usual hounding. Don't get me wrong, I didn't mind these pressure (as a matter of fact I loved it), it kept me on my toes all the time and I was always thinking. What I hated was the fact that they showed very little appreciation for all I did. It became very hard for me to tell people what I did and how much I made for my company without them judging me somehow. But it was fine, all these made it easy for me to make up my mind about leaving the company to become an entrepreneur.

When I sat to evaluate my situation, I discovered that I wasn't living in an apartment paid for by the firm, my car was mine and not official, I had no loan to pay back and my lifestyle wasn't expensive or luxurious in anyway. I weighed my options and after due consideration, I tendered my resignation in October 2015 and walked away from it all. I worked with this particular firm for a total of seven years.

Like I did before resigning my appointment at the aviation company, I projected 5 years into the future and I didn't like what I saw. Most star sales personnel go through this kind of experiences as well but they are usually too afraid to leave companies where they have once been celebrated as mavericks for new challenges for fear of the unknown. This is not a quality of a good sales person. We are bold, we are fearless, we are daring and very adventurous. That is why we are able to achieve the targets we set in the first place. This journey is not for the timid or lily livered. I'm writing this book four years after I resigned and I still have no regrets. I have taken on new challenges and even though I have had to tweak a few strategies here and there, I'm still here going strong and improving daily. Everything I have done, including writing this book, I doubt I would have been able to achieve, if I had remained in that firm.

CHAPTER 4

# QUALITIES OF A GOOD SALES PERSON

# QUALITIES OF A GOOD SALES PERSON

Selling is 80% mindset and 20% sales strategies and tactics. So, if your mindset is faulty, you will ultimately struggle to sell.

Growing up, I didn't like sales people, I resented them. I generally saw them as con men who were only interested in collecting your money by feeding you false information with their sweet lies. However, as I grew and started my first job, I realized that sales people are as important to the growth of any organization or economy as bees are to the survival of mankind. The business world is a battle ground; the side that sells is the side that wins.

To sell, you don't need to pressure someone to buy what you're selling. You're only required to share the information you have about your products or services truthfully and if your prospect sees value in the products, a sale is imminent. The point here is that good sales people are not con men. We don't force or manipulate prospects to buy what they need. If they feel pressured by you, they'll start avoiding you and you will lose the sale.

In case you wish to know the qualities you need to have to be a good and effective sales person, below are some real qualities that I totally agree with.

Some of them you can see in the story shared above and some I'm sure you have noticed in a sales person you greatly admire. The under listed was adopted from Rob Starr's article on smallbiztrends.com. The article is titled 'What Makes a Good Salesperson?

**QUALITIES OF GOOD SALES PERSONNEL:**
Ability to Listen A good salesperson needs to satisfy a client's needs and the only way to find out what those needs are is by listening to what each prospect is saying. I totally agree with this. No matter your profession, you would be a huge success if you can learn the art of listening instead of always wanting to talk. As human beings we are always so eager to talk without adequately

listening to what the other person is saying.

Please note here that you're not only listening for what the customer is saying but also for what they are not saying. i.e. their body language. By paying attention to this, you will know if a customer is buying your sales pitch or not and would be able to adjust quickly during presentations

**Empathy**

If you can feel what a person is feeling, you would always be able to help them find solutions to their problems (if you care enough). A good salesperson knows how to feel what their customers feel. The essence of empathy is not to be paralyzed by the customer's stories but to sift through their pain and find them products or services that would be able to help solve their challenges. Empathy is a great way to anticipate what a customer wants.

**Hunger**

I have always said that a salesman is a shameless person. It is not an insult but rather, a compliment. A good salesman does not let shame get in the way of his sale. He is too hungry for that. He has goals that must be attained and bills to pay. His need to sell is not all about money sometimes it's a confidence booster. A sales person has personal needs only a sale can help them with. In short, their egos need to be fed with good sales numbers.

**Competitiveness**
Sales people who succeed enjoy measuring their skills against their peers. In a word, they're competitiveness. They don't just want to get better at what they do. They want to be better than everyone else.

**Networking Ability**
You are only as good and efficient as your network. Good salespeople love to network. They get involved in their community and have many different business relationships. Networking is not so much a part of the job to them but the way they like to spend their time. Every time you find yourself struggling to make a sale check yourself, it just may be time for you to change or expand your current network.

**Confidence**
Your confidence level as a sales person increases with your knowledge of the product or service you're trying to

sell. You will find that every time a prospect knows more than you about a product, you will most likely lose that sale. Believing in the product or service you are selling is essential. Your belief in what you sell comes across as confidence to a customer and it generates an infectious vibe that makes customers want to buy more.

**Enthusiasm**

A successful salesperson is always motivated. You are able to sell only when you have successfully transferred your enthusiasm about a product or service to a prospective customer. This therefore means that you must always be of high spirit about what you're selling and be ready to make a sale at any given moment while continually looking for possibilities.

**Resilience**

Top earners know how to bounce back from a dry spell. They don't get discouraged when their sales numbers are down. Rather, they look for innovative ways to turn things around. If like me, you sell high luxury properties, you must know that closing deals most times will take time and that during economic recession; your job would be a lot tougher. Well, so must you. It takes me up to 3 years (or more) sometimes to get a client to buy a house. In my country, the mortgage system is non-existent so, you have to give people time to gather their funds and decide that its time for them to spend that much on a real estate investment rather than invest in their businesses or some other venture. You can't ever give up, this race is not for the faint at heart, it is for the resilient fighters that are prepared to always get back up and keep pushing.

**Multitasking Skills**

An outstanding salesperson knows how to juggle deals they are trying to close with promising leads. They can even respond to queries through emails and on the phone at the same time. You have to keep opening channels to be reached and initiating new leads. You have to find your range. You may need to pursue 10 leads to get one sale or 25 leads to get two or three (it all depends on a number of factors). Master your range and increase your list of prospects, this will always require you to multi task. Great multitaskers make excellent additions to any sales team.

## Honesty

Integrity is a bankable resource, the more people trust you, the more business you'll get. You don't want to be placed under the dishonest category of any customer. If they can't trust you, they can't and won't do business with you. Always paint the true picture about every product, leave the decision making to the client. Mention the pros and cons always so that your clients can make well informed decisions.

## Communications Skills

There is no way around having an excellent verbal skill if you wish to be a good sales person. People who excel here know how to stay away from jargon and hard to understand concepts. While speaking to a client, you must go straight to the point and avoid beating around the bush. While conversing, learn to read the faces and body movements of your prospects, you will get a lot of insights from this.

## Passion

When a sales representative loves their company, it shows in their pitch. That's why the most successful salespeople are the best cheerleaders for both the companies they work for and their private businesses. Like enthusiasm, passion is contagious and it is the fuel that keeps you going as a sales man/woman especially in really rough times. Protect your passion at all cost and ensure you don't burn out. Surround yourself with people, information and materials that keep you inspired and keeps your fire burning.

**Tenacity**

Sales person's job requires a lot of hard work because the weight of the company rests on their shoulders. The people who really succeed don't wait for customers to come to them; they go where the market is. The internet has made things a lot easier now but it is still not a walk in the park. Prospecting will take up a lot of your time as a sales person and you must understanding the concept of follow through.

**Charm**

Charming sales representatives create good first impressions that open the doors to sales. Working on your diction and having a groomed appearance makes a big difference. Smile, smell nice, look good, check your breath, learn the culture/language around you or of your prospects and watch what happens to your sales.

**Patience**

Like I mentioned earlier, it takes time to close on transactions at times. Some clients need a little more handling than others to close a sale. A good sales representative knows this and takes all the time needed. You must always have a buffer (cash reserve) so you don't become impatient and desperate about a transaction. Customers easily see this and it's a great turn off for them.

**Independence**

Being self-motivated and working on a commission makes the best salespeople really good at working on their own. Most organizations (especially in developing nations) will try to cheat you out of your commissions anyway (while they keep increasing your targets) so, why not choose your independence over all that chaos. At least this way, you have a lot more things in your control.

CHAPTER 5

# UNDERSTANDING THE SALSES PROCESSES

# UNDERSTANDING THE SALSES PROCESSES

Sales processes for the purpose of definition can be termed as the different stages a seller goes through in an attempt to achieve a sale. Like I mentioned earlier, selling is 80% a matter of the mind and 20% about how well you can follow sales processes and strategies. Since we have dealt with the attitude requirements of a good sales person, let's take a look at the processes.

Even though, sales processes may differ from company to company (depending on their products or services), for the benefit of this book we will be discussing some standard methods that have held true for many years.

**PROSPECTING**
Living in a populous nation like Nigeria is not an automatic sales guarantee. You need to sit down and carefully identify who your potential customers are. This is because

even if everyone likes your products and would love to have it, the truth is that not everyone would be able to afford it.

You must therefore identify the people who would see your product as good value for the price placed on it and are willing and able to purchase same at this moment. Prospecting is therefore, the process of finding and qualifying potential customers.

One of the easiest ways to do this is to identify an effective dragnet system to pull a large prospect base in so you can then filter the list down.

**GETTING READY**

Before contacting your prospects, you must ensure that you as the sales representative know all there is to know about the products or services you are trying to sell as you are only as effective as the information you have on the products.

For instance, if a prospect has some information (e.g. negative review) about your product, you would not be able to sell that customer is you don't have better information to counter this negative review. The getting ready stage is therefore the phase where youensure that you have all angles covered information wise. You collate and study all relevant information about the elements key to making your sales a success. i.e. your product/service information, competitors info etc. You can also get your sales pitch and presentation ready.

**THE MEETING**

After identifying your prospects and equipping yourself with all the necessary information about the product you're selling, the next step is to set up meetings with them. Most experienced sale representatives love to meet prospects. However, for the young and not too experienced sales people may get a little bit nervous about this. The main problem is always about not knowing how to start the conversation as well as the dos and don'ts of sales meetings.

To break the ice, you may need to consider out of the following approach styles:

1. **The premium approach:** This entails giving gifts like fancy pens
2. **The Question approach:** Asking the prospect critical

questions about their needs and using their responses as a soft landing to commence.
3. **The Product Approach:** Giving them samplesof your products to examine and asking for their opinions thereafter.

Depending on the situation on ground and the caliber of customers you're meeting with, you can choose which ever approach best soothes the setting and you can develop which ever style you feel works for you.

In addition to the above, ensure you are well dressed, maintain eye contact, shake hands firmly, put your phone on silent and don't waste time. You have about 2 minutes to make a good first impression and sell your product. Don't waste it.

**PRESENTATION**

While preparing your presentation, you must know what you are trying to achieve. Even though the ultimate goal is sales, your presentation gives you the opportunity to paint your desired pictures in the minds of your listeners. This where you make your audience see why they need your products and why your products are a better option than the competitors'. It is also a good opportunity to actively listen to the needs and wants of your potential clients and state how your product can meet them perfectly.

**DEALING WITH CRITICISMS AND OBJECTIONS**
Either during or after your presentation, there may be some very curious prospects who will ask some hard questions or tell you negative things they've heard or read about your products. You must learn to calm down and respond to these kind of people with respect and lots of wisdom. If you disagree with their views, state your points and make sure the conversation doesn't degenerate into an argument.

If there are criticisms about your presentation style or about the product, also take note and make adjustments (if personal) or inform your company about same so that improvements can be made.

**CLOSING**
Every work you do through the sales process is aimed at closing. Closing the sale is the goal of all your hard work and if you're good at closing, you will be very successful

as a sales man/woman. This involves identifying closing signals from your prospects and not being afraid to ask for their order/cheques.

It usually is not very straight forward as the customer may still have questions and objections (or ask for time to think about it) but if you did a good job with your presentation, then it should be quite simple.

**FOLLOW UP/FOLLOW THROUGH**

Usually, what happens at closing is that a buyer tells you of their intention to purchase from you and promises to make payment at a later date as purchase of your product was not in their plan or budget for the current month.

This is fine and very understandable. But you have to realize that the moment you leave that prospect, so many other sales people, adverts from television or social media will bombard him or her fighting for an equal (or more) share of his/her resources and he will start rationalizing his decision to either purchase your product or spend his budgeted funds on other products. This is what we call end games in chess. The buyer has decided in his mind to buy, but since human wants are numerous and their resources limited, the competition for whose products gets purchased becomes a really stiff one. The winner at this point is the sales man or woman who is a champion at the art of follow up and follow through.

Making payment is a very difficult decision to make and buyersunderstandable so,struggle to make this decision every time. As a matter of fact, most customers will conveniently forget their promises to you and pray that you forget as well. If you don't know how to call them up for reminders, stylishly visit for courtesy visit or devise other means to ensure you're constantly on their minds, your product purchase would be sacrificed for those of sales people who know how to follow through to make the sale

The way I see it, most sales representatives fail at follow through because they don't have things in proper perspective. Like I mentioned earlier in the book, shame is a luxury that a sales man or woman cannot afford. If you realize that the salaries of workers in your firm are dependent on your ability to sell and bring in money or that if you don't sell, your family may starve and lack the good things of life then you will understand that you cannot be ashamed of reminding a customer who has promised you payment of his promise to you or why buying your products is a better decision to make that purchasing other products or services.

CHAPTER 6

# MARKETING IS LIKE THROWING A PARTY

# MARKETING IS LIKE THROWING A PARTY

Marketing is like throwing a party. A man throws a party and invites everyone (both friends and strangers). Everyone comes and they are entertained. They are thrilled by the hospitality of their host and the image of the host is greatly enhanced. Most of the people at the party are probably strangers to the host at first but end up later becoming friends or acquaintances (strangers no more). They may have heard of the host in the past but this opportunity enables them to now meet him for the first time. They meet the host and decide from their experience at his party if they want to have a post party relationship with him or simple move on and remain strangers. This is very similar to what happens during marketing.

Dr. Sam Adeyemi, the Senior Pastor of Daystar Christian Center in Lagos Nigeria, recently shared the story of how he got an idea on how to increase membership of his church from 2,000 members to 5,000 members which later lead to the over 25,000 members they currently have. He explained how he got an idea while in the shower that he should organise his church services as if he was throwing a party.

That is it! That is what marketing is all about. Let's break it down.

When you are organising a party, these are the things you put in place:
1. A safe, comfortable and befitting venue for the caliber of people you what to invite/attract,
2. You make available good music and other forms of entertainment for your distinguished guests, so they're not bored while at your party. In the case of a church this comes in form of solid worship and impeccable music during the choir ministration or drama. Etc
3. Good food and drinks. In the case of a church, since people go to church to feed their spirit and soul, the food is fresh Revelation from God to the people through the word of God.
4. You put officials in place (ushers) to make sure that

the needs of every guest present are adequately attended to.
5. You create invites or invitation letters and you send the invites to as many people and you want to see at your party.
6. Before the party is over, the host goes round to thank the guests for coming and asks if there is anything they need. This is the same as vote of thanks.
7. You call attendees after the party to thank them for their attendance and support. This further solidifies your relationship with them (i.e. follow up).

Please look through the above activities carefully, how are these steps different from the typical steps for an effective marketing campaign?

There is no better activity to pull crowds like parties. It works like magic all the time.

**THE SALES FUNNEL**
Like the party illustration, the impressions made in the hearts of your target market during your marketing processes will determine a whole lot about whether or not they want to do business with you and keep you

at harms length. The Sales Funnel in marketing can therefore be defined as the path each of your potential customers take on their journey to making a purchase.

Even though it may seem complicated, it is actually a very simple.

It is a step by step process with the Top, Middle and Bottom of the Funnel. Designing your Sales Funnel as a Sales Person helps you track your progress and it helps you ensure that you are taking the right steps to ensure sales and limit disappointments. Even though Sales Funnels may vary from company to company depending on their sales model, below is a diagram of a typical Sales Funnel:

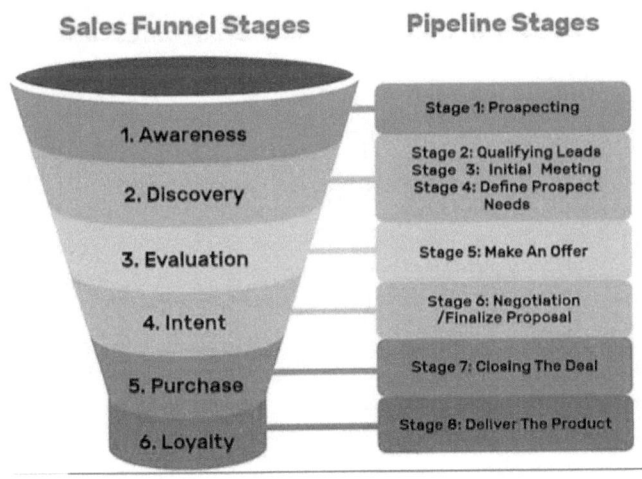

This diagram is not in any way different from the explanations made in the Sales Process segment above as it basically explains the steps listed in the diagram. What the Sales Funnel helps you achieve much more is identifying the level each of your prospective buyer is on their journey to making a purchase from you and what you need to do next.

# CONCLUSION

For organizations, I think it's very important for them to note that selling is not magic. You don't begin to automatically sell because you've employed some sales people. You need to do the right things to get the right results. All employees should be treated with respect and dignity but much more than this, organisations need to value their sales force and treat them right. Since theorganisational growth is largely dependent on the performance of the sales team, it's only logical and very important that you adequately empower them and ensure that your reward system show that you appreciate them.

The sales team also needs to be updated regularly with the right trainings and with access to the required resources for them to be productive.

The truth is that a career in sales isn't easy but neither is Engineering or any other profession at that. Those who succeed in their various professions and careers make up their mind that in addition to the passion and grace they have for such careers, they must add hard and consistent work. Like I have mentioned a number of times in this book, Sales is 80% a matter of the mind and 20% your compliance with laid down sales principles

Everyone who succeeds in sales knows that with persistence, patience and an ever burning enthusiastic spirit, their success is guaranteed. It may take a while, but it is certain. And like I always say;'if you can see true value in any product, service or idea, you will sell it to someone you love in no time because you are sure it will benefit them in one way or the other'. This is the summary of selling.

The question is; how come you find it hard to tell people (your loved ones included) about the products you have benefited from? Especially when you know that they need these products too. Could it be that you actually don't care enough about them, or you just don't love them enough to tell them?

If you really love them, it wouldn't be so hard for you to share information that could profit them even if you're the shy type. Think about it. In the end, I guess selling is not so hard, we just don't care enough.

www.ingramcontent.com/pod-product-compliance
Lightning Source LLC
Chambersburg PA
CBHW031545210526
45464CB00003B/1156